To Kill a Mock

L-I-T *Guide*
Literature In Teaching

By Harper Lee

A Study Guide for Grades 7 and up

Prepared by Rebecca Stark

Illustrated by Karen Neulinger

ISBN 1-56644-979-0 (10-digit)
978-1-56644-979-3 (13-digit)

Revised Edition:
© 2007 Educational Impressions, Inc., Hawthorne, NJ

EDUCATIONAL IMPRESSIONS, INC.
Hawthorne, NJ 07507

Printed in the United States of America.

To Kill a Mockingbird
Written by Harper Lee

STORY SUMMARY

This story is set in Alabama from 1933 to 1935. It is told in retrospect by Jean Louise (Scout) Finch, beginning with events that occurred when she was six years old and her brother Jem was ten.

There are two main plots. The first revolves around Arthur (Boo) Radley, a neighborhood recluse. Rumors about him abound, and Scout, Jem, and their friend Dill are involved in several games and pranks centering around him and their desire to get him out of his house. As the story progresses, the children begin to form their own opinions about Boo, who appears to be the source of several acts of kindness. They also come to realize that their earlier actions were insensitive and even cruel.

The second plot revolves around Scout and Jem's father, Atticus. Atticus is a lawyer defending Tom Robinson, a black man falsely accused of raping a white girl. Scout and Jem become aware of the prejudices and racism that exist. The miscarriage of justice that results from that racism has a great impact upon them both.

When the girl's drunken father, Bob Ewell, seeks revenge upon Atticus for defending Tom Robinson, the two plots come together. Bob Ewell attacks the children on their way home from a Halloween pageant. Arthur Radley kills Mr. Ewell and rescues the children. The sheriff, realizing that Arthur killed only in order to save the children and knowing that the ordeal of a trial would be too much for him, decides to report that Mr. Ewell fell on his own knife. By the time the story ends, both Scout and Jem have matured greatly!

Meet the Author
Harper Lee

Harper Lee, the youngest of three siblings, was born on April 28, 1926, in Monroeville, Alabama. Her parents were Amasa and Francis Finch Lee. From the time she was a young child, Harper loved to read. She attended local schools until 1944, when she enrolled in Huntington College in Montgomery. She attended Oxford University in England for a year as a Fullbright scholar. From 1945 to 1949 Harper studied law at the University of Alabama, but she withdrew before attaining her law degree.

In 1950 Ms. Lee moved to New York City. There she worked as an airline reservation clerk—first for Eastern Airlines and then for British Overseas Air Corporation, where she stayed for several years. Finally, she quit her job to devote all of her time to writing.

To Kill a Mockingbird was originally meant to be a series of short stories; however, Ms. Lee's agent persuaded her to expand the work into a complete novel. When she submitted it to J.B. Lippincott in 1957, the publisher thought it was still too much like a series of short stories. She rewrote it again! In 1960, the book was finally published. *To Kill a Mockingbird* was awarded the Pulitzer Prize for fiction in 1961. In 1962 it was released as an Oscar-winning movie starring Gregory Peck.

Harper Lee drew on her childhood experiences in writing *To Kill a Mockingbird*. Her father, Frances Finch Lee, was a lawyer. She modeled the character Atticus Finch after him. Many of the other characters, too, were based upon her recollection of people she had known growing up in the south. Maycomb, the fictional town where the story was set, greatly resembled Harper Lee's home town of Monroeville.

Although *To Kill a Mockingbird* was her only published novel, Harper Lee will always be remembered as a great American novelist. Indeed, her book has become a classic work of literature!

Pre-Reading Activity
Legal Terms

In this book you will come across many legal terms. Fill in the blanks with the appropriate terms from the box to complete these definitions. You may need to use your dictionary.

acquittal	appeal	contempt	convict
cross-examine	defendant	evidence	jury
litigant	prosecute	solicitor	subpoena
testify	testimony	verdict	venue

1. The locality from which a jury is called and in which a trial is held is the _____.

2. A(n) _____ is a legal writ requiring one's appearance in court.

3. A(n) _____ is a body of persons sworn to hear a case and hand down a verdict.

4. The chief law officer in a city, town, or government department is a(n) _____.

5. One who is engaged in a lawsuit is a(n) _____.

6. To _____ is to bear witness under oath.

7. One against whom an action is brought is a(n) _____.

8. _____ is a declaration of fact given before a court.

9. To question a witness already examined by the opposing side is to _____.

10. Open disrespect toward the authority of a court of law is _____.

11. _____ is statements, documents, and objects admissible as testimony.

12. To initiate legal or court action against someone is to _____.

13. The decision reached by a jury is the _____.

14. A(n) _____ is the judgment of a jury or judge that a person is not guilty.

15. To _____ is to request a transfer of a case to a higher court for a new trial.

16. To _____ is to find guilty by verdict of a court.

Vocabulary
Chapters One, Two, and Three

Match the vocabulary words on the left to the definitions on the right. Place the correct letter on each line.

_____ 1. assuage

_____ 2. condescend

_____ 3. contemptuous

_____ 4. cootie

_____ 5. disapprobation

_____ 6. dispensation

_____ 7. entailment

_____ 8. flivver

_____ 9. fractious

_____ 10. intimidation

_____ 11. malevolent

_____ 12. nebulous

_____ 13. prediliction

_____ 14. stealthy

_____ 15. taciturn

_____ 16. unsullied

_____ 17. vapid

_____ 18. vexation

A. an old or cheap car

B. vague

C. intended to escape observation

D. to ease; to make less painful

E. act of discouraging by threats

F. not stained; not tainted

G. to agree to do something beneath one's dignity

H. a preference

I. untalkative; uncommunicative

J. a baby louse

K. lacking zest or interest

L. a limit on an inheritance of property

M. an annoyance

N. scornful; feeling disdain

O. exhibiting ill will

P. moral disapproval

Q. inclined to make trouble

R. the act of giving out or dispensing

Choose four words from the first part of this activity. Use each in an original sentence.

_____

_____

_____

_____

_____

_____

Comprehension and Discussion Questions
Chapters One, Two, and Three

Answer the following questions in complete sentence form. Give examples from the story to support your response.

CHAPTER ONE:

1. Describe the techniques used by Harper Lee to tell the readers the story.

_____

_____

_____

_____

2. The time and place in which a story takes place is called its setting. Describe the setting of *To Kill a Mockingbird* as best as you can from reading the first chapter.

_____

_____

_____

_____

3. In this chapter the author prepares the readers for the attitudes and prejudices that create the mood that will prevail throughout the novel. Cite some examples.

_____

_____

_____

_____

4. How did Jem, Scout, and Dill entertain themselves? What did Dill encourage Jem and Scout to do when they got bored with those activities?

_____

_____

_____

_____

CHAPTER TWO:

1. Look up the meaning of ''satire.'' Use what you learn to show how the author used satire in describing Scout's experience with Miss Caroline Fisher.

_____

_____

_____

_____

2. Explain Scout's statement: "Walter hasn't got a quarter at home to bring you, and you can't use any stovewood."

_____

_____

_____

_____

3. How do you think you would have felt if you had been Miss Caroline?

_____

_____

_____

_____

CHAPTER THREE:

1. Compare and contrast Jem and Scout as evidenced by their treatment of Walter Cunningham.

_____

_____

_____

_____

2. In this chapter we met a member of the Ewell family. Do you think the Ewells will play an important role in upcoming chapters? Support your opinion.

_____

_____

_____

_____

3. Evaluate Atticus's advice to Scout: "You never really understand a person until you consider things from his point of view—until you climb into his skin and walk around in it."

_____

_____

_____

_____

4. Calpurnia was the Finches' housekeeper. Write a brief character sketch using information from the first three chapters to support your opinion.

_____

_____

_____

_____

5. What agreement did Scout and Atticus reach?

_____

_____

_____

_____

Vocabulary
Chapters Four, Five, and Six

Fill in the blanks with the appropriate words from the vocabulary box to complete these definitions. You may need to use your dictionary.

arbitrated	asinine	auspicious	contradicted	cordiality
edification	evasion	excluded	inquisitive	morbid
offended	parcel	pestilence	probate	quelling
quibble	ramshackle	scuppernogs	tacit	teetered

1. The _____ shed looked as if it would collapse.

2. The lessons provided _____ of the problem for the audience.

3. Bob and Jim could not agree, so Mary _____; they had to accept her judgment.

4. His _____ behavior embarrassed his friends.

5. The _____ resulted in many deaths.

6. _____ are his favorite kind of grapes.

7. She tried to avoid answering the question, but her father was aware of her _____.

8. Although she never said so, her behavior gave _____ approval of the plan.

9. It was John's job to _____ out the supplies; he gave each an equal amount.

10. She raised many trivial objections; the judge asked her not to _____.

11. The _____ judge said the will was valid.

12. Jack said they were almost there; Jane _____ him by saying they had miles to go.

13. The _____ child was curious about everything.

14. The wedding was a(n) _____ occasion.

15. The man's profanity _____ those around him.

Five of the words from the first part of this activity were not used. Use each in an original sentence.

_____

_____

_____

_____

_____

_____

Comprehension and Discussion Questions
Chapters Four, Five, and Six

Answer the following questions in complete sentence form. Give examples from the story to support your response.

CHAPTER FOUR:

1. Who, do you think, was leaving gifts for Jem and Scout?

_____

_____

_____

_____

2. Describe the game played by the children. Why, do you think, did Jem evade Atticus's question when Atticus asked what they were playing?

_____

_____

_____

_____

3. Why did Scout want to quit their game?

_____

_____

_____

_____

CHAPTER FIVE:

1. Why did Scout grow closer to Miss Maudie Atkinson. Explain the metaphor "chameleon lady."

_____

_____

_____

_____

2. What did Miss Maudie say that prompted Scout to defend her father? What did she say in his defense?

_____

_____

_____

_____

3. Judge the children's attempt to give a note to Boo. Do you think it was cruel? Explain.

_____

_____

_____

_____

4. "Jem...realized that he had been done in by the oldest lawyer's trick on record." Explain.

_____

_____

_____

_____

CHAPTER SIX:

1. What went wrong in Jem and Dill's plot to peep in the window to try to get a look at Boo Radley?

_____

_____

_____

_____

2. Explain the importance of Mr. Radley's assumption that a Negro was in his collard patch.

_____

_____

_____

_____

3. Why was it significant that Jem was determined to return alone to the Radley residence to retrieve his pants?

_____

_____

_____

_____

Vocabulary
Chapters Seven, Eight, and Nine

Choose the word or phrase in each set that is **most like** the first word in meaning.

1. **aberration:** trend deviation abbreviation

2. **accost:** ignore neglect address

3. **ascertain:** determine dismiss climb

4. **compensation:** revenge competition payment

5. **deportment:** division behavior expulsion

6. **lineament:** feature ancestry kindred

7. **perpetrate** commit last bewilder

8. **procure:** give obtain fix

9. **provocation:** warning award incitement

10. **stalk:** pursue grow claim

Choose the word or phrase in each set that is **most unlike** the first word in meaning.

11. **abusive:** disrespectful respectful harsh

12. **analogous:** dissimilar similar bitter

13. **dire:** promising extreme dreadful

14. **fanatical:** zealous indifferent excessive

15. **guileless:** deceitful honest naive

16. **inevitable:** unavoidable certain avoidable

17. **innate:** inborn inherent acquired

18. **obstreperous:** noisy quiet mean

19. **uncompromising:** stubborn unfair flexible

20. **unfathomable:** understandable mysterious deep

Comprehension and Discussion Questions
Chapters Seven, Eight, and Nine

Answer the following questions in complete sentence form. Give examples from the story to support your response.

CHAPTER SEVEN:

1. What surprise did Jem encounter when he returned to the Radley Place to retrieve his pants? Why did it upset him? Guess who was responsible and the possible significance.

_____

_____

_____

_____

2. List all the gifts put in the tree for the children.

_____

_____

_____

_____

3. Jem was obviously disturbed by the fact that Mr. Radley had filled the hole in the tree with cement. Why, do you think, did he appear more upset than Scout?

_____

_____

_____

_____

CHAPTER EIGHT:

1. Why did Scout believe that the world was coming to an end?

_____

_____

_____

_____

2. According to Mr. Avery, who was to blame for the harsh winter? What was his source of information?

_____

_____

_____

_____

3. Mr. Avery either did not know, or chose to ignore, the real meaning of the Rosetta Stone. Find out what the Rosetta Stone was and explain.

4. What can you gather from Scout's use of the word ''nigger''?

5. Why did Atticus suggest that the children ''disguise'' their snowman?

6. Who put the blanket around Scout? Comment on the importance of this fact.

7. How did Miss Maudie react to the loss of her house?

CHAPTER NINE:

1. For the first eight chapters, the plot focused around Boo Radley. In this chapter we were introduced to another plot—one involving Tom Robinson. Explain who Tom Robinson was and his relationship to Atticus Finch.

2. What prompted Atticus to advise Scout, ''You just hold your head high and keep those fists down''?

3. Analyze Atticus's statement: ''Simply because we were licked a hundred years before we started is no reason for us not to try to win.''

_____

_____

_____

_____

4. Why did Scout imagine that her Aunt Alexandra was a changeling?

_____

_____

_____

_____

5. Using Francis and Scout as examples, whose method of upbringing do you think was more successful, Aunt Alexandra's or Atticus's?

_____

_____

_____

_____

6. Toward the end of this chapter the author used foreshadowing to give us a hint of trouble to come. Cite one or two examples.

_____

_____

_____

_____

7. What did Atticus mean by ''Maycomb's usual disease''?

_____

_____

_____

_____

Vocabulary
Chapters Ten and Eleven

From the words in the vocabulary box, select the word that best completes each analogy. You may need to use your dictionary.

---

addict	apopletic	cantankerous	compassion
feeble	inconspicuous	interdict	livid
melancholy	palliation	propensity	rectitude
tartly	tirade	umbrage	wrathful

---

1. _____ is to weak as arid is to dry.

2. Noticeable is to _____ as low is to high.

3. _____ is to sweetly as carefully is to carelessly.

4. Sorrow is to grief as _____ is to resentment.

5. _____ is to righteousness as loyalty is to faithfulness.

6. _____ is to prohibition as edict is to law.

7. Quarrelsome is to _____ as stubborn is to obstinate.

8. Desire is to craving as _____ is to inclination.

9. _____ is to delighted as furious is to pleased.

10. Thankfulness is to gratitude as _____ is to sympathy.

11. _____ is to speech as edict is to decree.

12. Sad is to _____ as happy is to cheerful.

Four of the words from the first part of this activity were not used. Create an analogy for each.

_____

_____

_____

_____

_____

_____

_____

Comprehension and Discussion Questions
Chapters Ten and Eleven

Answer the following questions in complete sentence form. Give examples from the story to support your response.

CHAPTER TEN:

1. Atticus gave the children air rifles and with them some very important advice. Relate that advice and explain the significance of the mockingbird.

_____

_____

_____

_____

2. At the beginning of this chapter, the children seemed to be somewhat ashamed of Atticus. Why?

_____

_____

_____

_____

3. What happened in this chapter to change the children's opinion of Atticus?

_____

_____

_____

_____

4. How did the children's reactions to Atticus's shooting the dog differ?

_____

_____

_____

_____

CHAPTER ELEVEN:

1. Jem tried very hard to live up to Atticus's standards of being a gentleman. How did Mrs. Dubose provoke Jem into cutting the tops off her camelia bushes and breaking Scout's baton?

_____

_____

_____

_____

2. The following statement described Mrs. Dubose's tirade: "We were followed...by a philippic on our family's moral degeneration." Define the word "philippic" and explain the historical origins of the word. Use your dictionary if necessary.

_____

_____

_____

_____

3. Explain Atticus's statement: "The one thing that doesn't abide by majority rule is a person's conscience." Do you agree?

_____

_____

_____

_____

4. What commitment did Jem make to atone for the destruction of Mrs. Dubose's property?

_____

_____

_____

_____

5. How did Atticus respond to Scout's question of whether or not he was a "nigger-lover"?

_____

_____

_____

_____

6. Jem's growing maturity was evidenced by his response to Mrs. Dubose's statement: "Don't guess you feel like holding it [his head] up, though, with your father what he is." Explain.

_____

_____

_____

_____

7. What did we learn that explained Mrs. Dubose's fits?

_____

_____

_____

_____

8. According to Atticus, why did Mrs. Dubose's actions show great courage? How did this relate to Atticus's own situation?

_____

_____

_____

_____

Vocabulary
Chapters Twelve, Thirteen, and Fourteen

For each sentence circle the word that best completes the definition for the word printed in bold. Use your dictionary to help you. The first has been done for you.

1. An **altercation** is a _____.

    quarrel   change   option

2. An **amanuensis** is someone who _____ manuscript.

    creates   copies   edits

3. A **contentious** person is _____.

    quarrelsome   pleasant   compassionate

4. A **curt** response is _____.

    abrupt   long   humorous

5. To do something **diligently** is to do it with _____.

    ease   persistence   amusement

6. One meaning of **formidable** is _____.

    awesome   intense   formal

7. **Habiliments** are _____.

    customs   clothes   habits

8. **Impedimenta** are objects that _____.

    help   frighten   hinder

9. An **indignant** person believes something is _____.

    unjust   funny   difficult

10. A **pensive** person is _____ in a serious way.

    thinking   acting   talking

11. A **prerogative** is a _____.

    right   complaint   requirement

12. **Qualm** denotes a sensation of _____.

    fear   doubt   certainty

13. To **rankle** is to cause _____.

    irritation   dread   amusement

Comprehension and Discussion Questions
Chapters Twelve, Thirteen, and Fourteen

Answer the following questions in complete sentence form. Give examples from the story to support your response.

CHAPTER TWELVE:

1. What information do we learn about conditions in Alabama in 1935? Why might this information be significant to the plot?

_____

_____

_____

_____

2. Explain how the First Purchase African M.E. Church got its name. Describe the means by which the congregation sang the hymns. Why was this necessary?

_____

_____

_____

_____

3. Why did Reverend Sykes say, ''Nobody leaves here till we have ten dollars''? What does this tell us about the black community?

_____

_____

_____

_____

4. Analyze Calpurnia's remark: ''It's not necessary to tell all you know.''

_____

_____

_____

_____

CHAPTER THIRTEEN:

1. How did the author use foreshadowing while explaining the reason for Aunt Alexandra's stay with them?

_____

_____

_____

_____

2. Atticus lectured the children about trying to live up to their name. Why did this upset Scout and Jem?

_____

_____

_____

_____

3. The author used foreshadowing near the end of this chapter. Explain.

_____

_____

_____

_____

CHAPTER FOURTEEN:

1. When Alexandra said, "You've got to do something about her," to whom did she refer? What did she want Atticus to do? How did Atticus react?

_____

_____

_____

_____

2. What did Jem do that "broke the remaining code of [their] childhood"? Judge his decision to take that action.

_____

_____

_____

_____

3. Explain what Atticus meant when he told Dill to "put some of the county back where it belongs."

_____

_____

_____

_____

4. According to Dill, why did he run away? Why was this reason difficult for Scout to comprehend?

_____

_____

_____

_____

5. Dill constantly made up tall tales. Guess why.

_____

_____

_____

_____

Vocabulary
Chapters Fifteen, Sixteen, and Seventeen

For each set, tell which of the following relationships applies.

A.   a noun and its synonym
B.   a noun and its antonym
C.   a verb and its synonym
D.   a verb and its antonym

E.   an adjective and its synonym
F.   an adjective and its antonym
G.   an adverb and its synonym
H.   an adverb and its antonym

EXAMPLE:
(F)   happy is to sad
(D)   depart is to arrive

_____ 1. acrimonius is to bitter

_____ 2. affluent is to poor

_____ 3. aggregation is to assemblage

_____ 4. complacent is to discontent

_____ 5. connivance is to conspiracy

_____ 6. convene is to meet

_____ 7. corroborate is to support

_____ 8. deliberately is to carelessly

_____ 9. detractors is to supporters

_____ 10. devoid is to lacking

_____ 11. dictum is to pronouncement

_____ 12. elucidate is to explain

_____ 13. encumber is to assist

_____ 14. faintly is to weakly

_____ 15. gala is to somber

_____ 16. litigant is to suer

_____ 17. ominous is to menacing

_____ 18. scrutiny is to examination

_____ 19. smugness is to complacency

_____ 20. tenet is to principle

_____ 21. venerable is to honorable

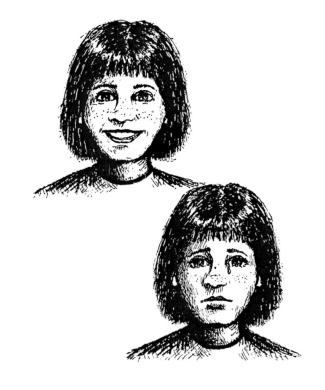

Comprehension and Discussion Questions
Chapters Fifteen, Sixteen, and Seventeen

Answer the following questions in complete sentence form. Give examples from the story to support your response.

CHAPTER FIFTEEN:

1. Conclude why Mr. Tate said, ''Change of venue. Not much point in that, now is it?''

_____

_____

_____

_____

2. The author used foreshadowing in the beginning of the chapter to give the readers a clue as to what would happen at the end of the chapter. Explain.

_____

_____

_____

_____

3. What prompted Jem to go downtown?

_____

_____

_____

_____

4. Compare and contrast the crowd of men who gathered outside the Finch home to those who gathered in front of the jail.

_____

_____

_____

_____

5. What happened to break the tension of the mob?

_____

_____

_____

_____

6. Atticus did not reprimand Jem for disobeying his instructions to go home. Why not?

_____

_____

_____

_____

CHAPTER SIXTEEN:

1. How did Jem's behavior toward Scout show his growing maturity?

_____

_____

_____

_____

2. Explain the reference to William Jennings Bryan.

_____

_____

_____

_____

3. Miss Maudie compared the atmosphere surrounding the trial to a Roman carnival. Why?

_____

_____

_____

_____

4. Miss Maudie used sarcasm when asking Miss Stephanie about going to the courthouse. Explain.

_____

_____

_____

_____

5. Scout overheard a conversation among the members of the Idlers' Club. What did she learn that put a "different light on things"? Why did this confuse her?

_____

_____

_____

_____

6. With whom did Scout, Jem, and Dill view the court proceedings?

_____

_____

_____

_____

CHAPTER SEVENTEEN:

1. If you had been on the jury, what would you have thought about the fact that no one had called a doctor to examine Mayella?

_____

_____

_____

_____

2. When Mr. Tate testified that Mayella Ewell had been beaten on her right side, something became clear to both Mr. Tate and Atticus. Predict what that might be.

_____

_____

_____

3. Characterize the Ewells.

_____

_____

_____

4. Why did Atticus ask Mr. Ewell to write his name?

_____

_____

_____

5. Scout became nervous when Atticus asked Mr. Ewell if he could write his name. Why?

_____

_____

_____

_____

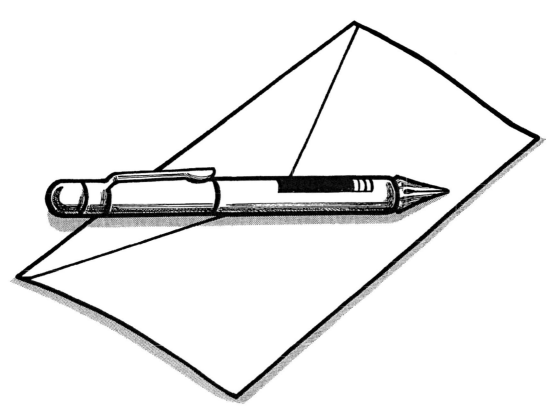

Vocabulary
Chapters Eighteen, Nineteen, and Twenty

Alphabetize the words in the box. Then find the words (or forms of the words) in these chapters. Use your dictionary to define them as they were used in the story.

chiffarobe	mollified	temerity	circumstantial	offense
expunge	corrupting	contradicting	unmitigated	corroborative
contorted	irrelevant	cynical	leveler	articulate
prejudice	detached	tedious	misdemeanor	candid

1.
2.
3.
4.
5.
6.
7.
8.
9.
10.
11.
12.
13.
14.
15.
16.
17.
18.
19.
20.

You Are There!

Pretend that you are a reporter living in Alabama in 1935. Report about the trial of Tom Robinson. Use eight or more vocabulary words in your story.

Comprehension and Discussion Questions
Chapters Eighteen, Nineteen, and Twenty

Answer the following questions in complete sentence form. Give examples from the story to support your response.

CHAPTER EIGHTEEN:

1. Cite evidence that Mayella was different from the other Ewells.

_____
_____
_____
_____

2. Why did Mayella think that Atticus was making fun of her?

_____
_____
_____
_____

3. What pertinent fact did we learn about Tom Robinson's physical condition?

_____
_____
_____
_____

4. Atticus tried to point the guilt in another direction. Whom did he suspect?

_____
_____
_____
_____

5. If you had been on the jury, would you have had doubts regarding Tom Robinson's guilt? Explain.

_____
_____
_____
_____

CHAPTER NINETEEN:

1. Characterize Tom Robinson from what you learned in this chapter.

_____
_____
_____
_____

2. What did Scout mean by the following: ''She was even lonelier than Boo Radley''?

_____

_____

_____

3. How did Tom's testimony about the evening of November 21 differ from Mayella's?

_____

_____

_____

4. Atticus was not the only white man to stand up for Tom. Who else spoke out in Tom's behalf?

_____

_____

_____

5. Tom regretted his explanation of why he helped Mayella. Explain.

_____

_____

_____

_____

6. How did Dill show his sensitivity?

_____

_____

_____

_____

CHAPTER TWENTY:

1. What did Mr. Dolphus Raymond mean by the following: ''You little folks won't tell on me now, will you? It'd ruin my reputation if you did''?

_____

_____

_____

_____

2. Why did Mr. Raymond entrust the children with his secret? What pessimism did he express?

_____

_____

_____

_____

3. Evaluate Atticus's closing statements. If you had been on the jury, would he have convinced you of Tom's innocence? Explain.

_____

_____

_____

_____

4. According to Atticus, Mayella was motivated to lie to rid herself of her guilt. What rigid code of her society did she break?

_____

_____

_____

_____

5. According to Atticus, the prosecutor's case was based upon "an evil assumption." Explain.

_____

_____

_____

_____

6. What did Atticus mean by "the distaff side of the Executive branch"?

_____

_____

_____

_____

7. Analyze Atticus's statements: "Courts are the great levelers" and "A court is no better than each man of you sitting before me on this jury."

_____

_____

_____

_____

8. Predict why Calpurnia interrupted the court session.

_____

_____

_____

_____

Vocabulary
Chapters Twenty-One, Twenty-Two, and Twenty-Three

Use your dictionary to define the following words. Then use the words and their definitions to create a crossword puzzle.

adamant	colleague	commute (a sentence)	credibility	diction
exhilarated	fatalistic	feral	fret	furtive
grudge	indignant	polling	relenting	reluctant
remorse	resentment	ruefully	sordid	statute
stolidly	tacit	tactics	wallow	wryly

Create a Crossword Puzzle

Use the vocabulary words from the first part of this activity to create a crossword puzzle. Try to use all of them! Write the clues on another piece of paper. Number the boxes horizontally and vertically. Darken the boxes that you are not using. Exchange with a classmate to solve!

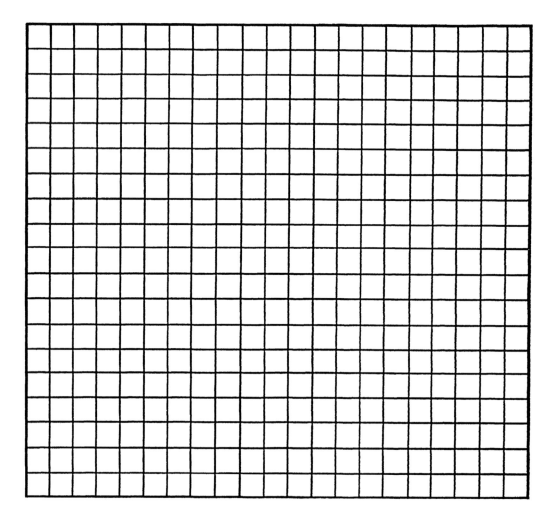

Comprehension and Discussion Questions
Chapters Twenty-One, Twenty-Two, and Twenty-Three

Answer the following questions in complete sentence form. Give examples from the story to support your response.

CHAPTER TWENTY-ONE:

1. Jem misinterpreted Atticus's statement, ''But I expect it'll be over before you get back.'' Explain.

_____

_____

_____

_____

2. As Scout awaited the return of the jury, she was overcome with a certain impression. It reminded her of an impression she had had the winter before. Explain.

_____

_____

_____

_____

3. What clue made Scout believe that the verdict would be guilty?

_____

_____

_____

_____

4. Why did Reverend Sykes ask Scout to stand?

_____

_____

_____

_____

CHAPTER TWENTY-TWO:

1. Compare Atticus's response to Jem's question ''How could they do it?'' to Dolphus Raymond's reason for telling the children his secret in Chapter Twenty.

_____

_____

_____

_____

2. Why did Atticus say that they weren't through yet?

_____

_____

_____

_____

3. Miss Maudie made a gesture that implied that to her, Jem had matured greatly. Explain.

_____

_____

_____

_____

4. According to Miss Maudie, who also had helped Tom Robinson?

_____

_____

_____

_____

5. According to Miss Maudie, what ray of optimism could be found in the outcome of the trial?

_____

_____

_____

_____

6. What news did Miss Stephanie tell the children?

_____

_____

_____

_____

CHAPTER TWENTY-THREE:

1. In Chapter Three, Atticus gave Scout advice about how to understand a person. In this chapter, he used similar advice to explain to Jem why he wasn't going to "do something about" Bob Ewell's threatening behavior. Explain.

_____

_____

_____

_____

2. What was it about the statute that bothered Atticus?

_____

_____

_____

_____

3. Atticus showed pride in Jem's power of observation. Explain.

_____

_____

_____

4. What surprising news did Atticus tell Jem about the jury in the Robinson case?

_____

_____

_____

5. Summarize what Aunt Alexandra said that caused Jem to say, "Scout, don't let Aunty aggravate you"?

_____

_____

_____

_____

Vocabulary
Chapters Twenty-Four, Twenty-Five, Twenty-Six, and Twenty-Seven

For each, circle the most appropriate definition for the word printed in bold as it is used in the sentence (which was excerpted from the story). Use your dictionary to help you. The first has been done for you.

1. August was on the **brink** of September.
   a. The upper edge of a slope
   b. The margin of land bordering a body of water
   c. The verge of something

2. They...spat out the bark...into a **communal** pot.
   a. Pertaining to a commune
   b. Belonging to the people of a community; public
   c. Pertaining to a small group of people who share property and duties

3. The ladies **adjourned** for refreshments.
   a. To move from one place to another
   b. To suspend until a later stated time
   c. To suspend proceedings to another place

4. Ladies in bunches always filled me with vague **apprehension.**
   a. Uneasy anticipation of the future
   b. The act of seizing or capturing
   c. The ability to understand

5. For certainly Mrs. Merriweather was the most **devout** lady in Maycomb.
   a. Sincere
   b. Deeply religious
   c. Displaying reverence

6. "...You have no **conception** of what we are fighting over there."
   a. A beginning
   b. A plan, design, or concept
   c. The ability to understand mental concepts

7. "...We're paying the highest **tribute** we can pay a man. We trust him to do right."
   a. A payment made for protection
   b. An acknowledgment of respect or admiration
   c. A tax given by a feudal vassal to his overlord

8. I sometimes feel a **twinge** of remorse....
   a. A sharp, sudden physical pain
   b. To pinch
   c. A mental or emotional pain

9. ...So the **burden** of Current Events was borne by the town children....
   a. To load or overload
   b. A responsibility or duty
   c. Something difficult to bear

For each of the following sentences, decide whether or not the meaning of the word in bold is the same as or different from its usage in the first part of this activity. If it is different, write the letter that corresponds to the correct usage.

1. He walked to the **brink** of the cliff and stopped. _____

2. The children swam in the **communal** pool. _____

3. The meeting was **adjourned** until next week. _____

4. The **apprehension** of the escaped convict was swift. _____

5. The card expressed **devout** wishes for the couple's happy marriage. _____

6. The architect had a **conception** of how the building would look. _____

7. The award was a **tribute** to his great courage. _____

8. The elderly lady got a **twinge** in her shoulder. _____

9. The **burden** of proof was on the prosecution. _____

Comprehension and Discussion Questions
Chapters Twenty-Four, Twenty-Five, Twenty-Six, and Twenty-Seven

Answer the following questions in complete sentence form. Give examples from the story to support your response.

CHAPTER TWENTY-FOUR:

1. Explain the irony in the missionary circle's concern with the "squalid lives of the Mrunas."

_____

_____

_____

_____

2. Why did Scout assume that Mrs. Merriweather was talking about Mayella when she said, "Well, I always say forgive and forget..."?

_____

_____

_____

_____

3. What caused Aunt Alexandra to give Miss Maudie a look of pure gratitude?

_____

_____

_____

_____

4. Scout expressed the idea that she preferred the company of her father and his friends. What did she mean by the following: "Mr. Heck Tate did not trap you with innocent questions to make fun of you"?

_____

_____

_____

5. Why did Atticus interrupt the gathering of the missionary circle to ask Calpurnia to accompany him?

_____

_____

_____

_____

6. Atticus said, "I told him what I thought, but I couldn't in truth say that we had more than a good chance." Judge Atticus's decision not to promise Tom more than "a good chance."

_____

_____

_____

_____

7. In this chapter, we saw Aunt Alexandra's character develop more fully. Explain.

_____

_____

_____

_____

8. How had Scout's attitude towards Aunt Alexandra changed?

_____

_____

_____

_____

CHAPTER TWENTY-FIVE:

1. Jem stopped Scout from killing a roly-poly. Relate this to the major theme of the book.

_____

_____

_____

_____

2. The symbol of the mockingbird appeared once again in this chapter. Explain.

_____

_____

_____

_____

3. Analyze the statement: "In the secret courts of men's hearts Atticus had no case."

_____

_____

_____

_____

4. There is an uneasy feeling at the end of this chapter. What caused it?

_____

_____

_____

_____

CHAPTER TWENTY-SIX:

1. Scout showed evidence of her growing maturity when she felt a "twinge of remorse" when passing by the Radley Place. Explain.

_____

_____

_____

_____

2. What was ironic about Miss Gate's harsh censure of Hitler's persecution of the Jews?

_____

_____

_____

_____

3. Analyze Jem's inability to discuss anything to do with the court house.

_____

_____

_____

_____

CHAPTER TWENTY-SEVEN:

1. What three things happened to further frustrate Bob Ewell?

_____

_____

_____

2. NRA is an acronym for the National Recovery Act. To whom did Atticus refer when he said that "nine old men" killed the NRA?

_____

_____

_____

3. There was a feeling of apprehension at the end of this chapter. What elements helped create this mood?

_____

_____

_____

_____

Vocabulary
Chapters Twenty-Eight, Twenty-Nine, Thirty, and Thirty-One

Read each clue and find the answers in the box. Then use the letters above the numbered spaces to decipher the secret message. Some of the words will not be used.

alleged	blandly	connive	disengage	entangle
garish	hock	instinctive	irascible	lectern
persevere	pinion	rale	rout	smocking
squander	teeming	trudge	untrammeled	venture

1. easily angered __ __ __ __ __ __ __ __ __
   ₃ ... ₁₈

2. to restrain by binding arms __ __ __ __ __ __
   ₇ ... ₁₇

3. decorative needlework __ __ __ __ __ __ __
   ₁₀ ₁₉

4. loud and flashy __ __ __ __ __ __
   ₂₂ ₂₄

5. not confined nor hindered __ __ __ __ __ __ __ __ __ __ __
   ₂ ₁₄

6. with no distinctive character __ __ __ __ __ __ __
   ₂₃ ₅

7. to free or detach oneself __ __ __ __ __ __ __ __
   ₂₆ ₁₂

8. to remain constant to a task __ __ __ __ __ __ __ __ __
   ₄

9. full of; abounding __ __ __ __ __ __ __
   ₁₆

10. to plot; to conspire __ __ __ __ __ __ __
    ₂₀

11. spontaneous and unthinking __ __ __ __ __ __ __ __ __ __ __
    ₈ ₁

12. speaker's stand __ __ __ __ __ __ __
    ₁₃ ₉

13. to spend wastefully __ __ __ __ __ __ __ __
    ₆ ₂₁

14. leg joint of 4-footed animal __ __ __ __
    ₁₁

15. to defeat; to cause to retreat __ __ __ __
    ₂₅

16. to make a rattling sound in throat __ __ __ __
    ₁₅

```
      1   2     3   4     5     6   7   8     9   10
__  __   __  __    __    __  __  __    __  __

11  12  13  14     15    16  17  18  19  20  21  22  23  24  25  26
__  __  __  __     __    __  __  __  __  __  __  __  __  __  __  __ •
```

Comprehension and Discussion Questions
Chapters Twenty-Eight, Twenty-Nine, Thirty, and Thirty-One

Answer the following questions in complete sentence form. Give examples from the story to support your response.

CHAPTER TWENTY-EIGHT:

1. The apprehensive mood continued in this chapter. Cite details that contributed to this mood before the attack on the children.

2. Why, do you think, did Aunt Alexandra bring Scout her overalls rather than a dress?

3. Guess who brought Jem inside.

4. Describe Jem's condition after the attack.

5. What important news did Mr. Tate reveal at the end of the chapter?

CHAPTER TWENTY-NINE:

1. Why did Aunt Alexandra feel guilty about the attack on the children? How would you have felt in her situation?

_____

_____

_____

_____

2. What prompted Mr. Tate to say, "We'll have to make him [Jem] a deputy"?

_____

_____

_____

3. Who brought Jem into the house? Did you guess correctly in the last chapter?

_____

_____

_____

_____

CHAPTER THIRTY:

1. How did Scout show kindness to Boo?

_____

_____

_____

_____

2. What conclusion did Atticus jump to regarding the death of Bob Ewell?

_____

_____

_____

3. Who really killed Bob Ewell? What evidence makes you think this?

_____

_____

_____

4. Whose kitchen knife was it? Whose switchblade was it? Why did Mr. Tate say that he had taken the switchblade off a drunk earlier that evening?

_____

_____

_____

5. Scout showed maturity by taking advice her father had given her and applying it to this situation. Explain.

_____

_____

_____

_____

CHAPTER THIRTY-ONE:

1. How did Scout continue to show compassion to Boo?

_____

_____

_____

_____

2. Whom do you think the Gray Ghost symbolized? Find the sentence that makes you think this.

_____

_____

_____

_____

3. What helped Scout "stand in Boo Radley's shoes"?

_____

_____

_____

_____

Spotlight Literary Skill
Theme and Spotlight

THEME

A **theme** is a central idea in a story. It should not be confused with the series of events, or the plot, of a story. One important theme of *To Kill a Mockingbird* is the need for human compassion. Another is the importance of individual conscience.

Think about these two themes. Find examples of each in the story.

THEME #1: *The Need for Human Compassion*

_____

_____

_____

_____

_____

THEME #2: *The Importance of Individual Conscience*

_____

_____

_____

_____

_____

SYMBOLISM

Symbolism is the use of an object, event, or relationship to represent something else. The most important symbol in *To Kill a Mockingbird* is the mockingbird.

What does the mockingbird represent?

_____

_____

_____

Cite examples in the story that support your answer.

_____

_____

_____

_____

_____

Cooperative Learning Activity
Life in the 1930's

This novel is set in Alabama from 1933 to 1935. With your cooperative-learning group, research what life was like during that period of time in the southern region of the United States. Some things to consider are economic conditions, the political situation, social programs, transportation, sports, entertainment, and fashion.

Compare your findings with those of the other groups.

Character Quest

Use the character names found in the box below to solve each of the following quotation questions:

Who made the statement?   *To whom* was it made?   *Why* was it made?

Atticus	Scout	Jem	Aunt Alexandra	Mr. Avery	Calpurnia
	Mrs. Dubose	Miss Maudie	Mr. Gilmer	Miss Caroline	
Tom Robinson	Dolphus Raymond		Heck Tate	Mayella Ewell	Boo Radley	Dill

1. "Now you tell your father not to teach you any more.... You'll tell him I'll take over from here and try to undo the damage—"

_____

_____

2. "Hush your mouth! Don't matter who they are, any body sets foot in this house's yo' company...."

_____

_____

3. "You never really understand a person...until you climb into his skin and walk around in it."

_____

_____

4. "It's bad children like you makes the seasons change."

_____

_____

5. "Shoot all the bluejays you want...but remember it's a sin to kill a mockingbird."

_____

_____

6. "I wanted you to see what real courage is....It's when you know you're licked before you begin but you begin anyway and you see it through no matter what."

_____

_____

7. "Yes, suh. I fel right sorry for her, she seemed to try more'n the rest of 'em—"

_____

_____

8. "Things haven't caught up with that one's instinct yet. Let him get a little older and he won't get sick and cry."

_____

_____

9. "There's a black boy dead for no reason, and the man responsible for it's dead. Let the dead bury the dead this time...."

_____

_____

To Kill a Mockingbird 45

Crossword Puzzle
To Kill a Mockingbird

See how much you remember about *To Kill a Mockingbird.* Have fun!

Across

1. Fictional town where story is set.
3. State where story takes place.
7. What Jim must do for Mrs. Dubose.
8. Friend of Scout and Jim.
10. Atticus's brother.
11. Scout's brother.
12. Atticus's sister.
14. Atticus shoots one.
15. Attacks Jem.
17. Finch family's housekeeper.
19. Dolphus Raymond pretends to be this.
22. Narrates the story.
23. Holiday on which children are attacked.
24. Last name of Atticus, Scout, and Jem.

Down

1. Her house burns down.
2. She overcomes her morphine addiction.
4. Recluse who saves Jim.
5. Scout's age when the story begins.
6. Scout's teacher.
9. Sheriff of Maycomb.
11. Scout's real name.
13. Falsely accused of rape.
16. Author of *To Kill a Mockingbird.*
18. Defends Tom Robinson in court.
20. Falsely accuses Tom Robinson.
21. Judge handling Tom's case.

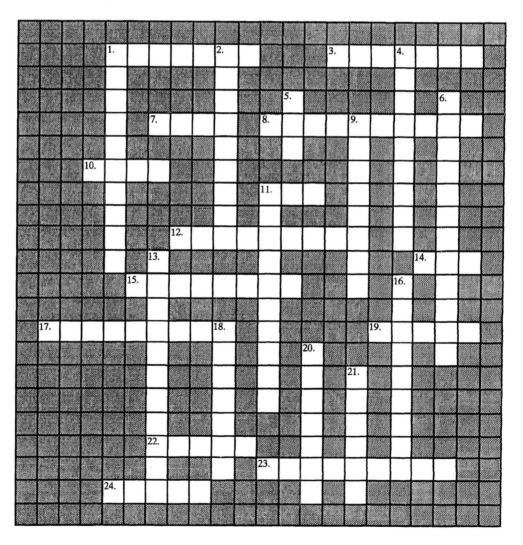

Post-Reading Activities

1. Make a chart that traces Scout's maturity.

2. Suppose Arthur "Boo" Radley had been brought to trial. With your class or with members of your cooperative-learning group, role-play that trial.

3. Write a letter to the editor of your local newspaper describing your feelings after the jury pronounced Tom guilty.

4. Investigate and report on what life was like for blacks living in the South in the 1930's.

5. Write about an experience you or someone you know has had involving prejudice and/or discrimination.

6. Create a board game based upon events and characters in the novel.

7. View the film version of *To Kill a Mockingbird*, starring Gregory Peck. Does it differ in any way from the book? If so, tell how.

8. As casting director for a remake of the film, decide whom you would like to cast in each part. Write a letter to the producer explaining your choices.

9. Design a poster to encourage others to read this book.

10. Make a list of other animals that might have been used as a symbol instead of the mockingbird.

11. The United Nations declared 1995 the Year of Tolerance. The following is an excerpt from that declaration: "It is essential to understand that while all are equal in dignity, all are different in terms of their talents, convictions and beliefs, and these differences are a factor of enrichment for every individual and for civilization as a whole." Collect pictures, magazine articles, etc., to create a scrapbook using this statement as a theme.

12. Choose an episode from the book and re-write it from another character's point of view.

13. Create titles for each of the chapters.

14. In Chapter 14 Dill told a tall tale to explain how he got to the Finch house. Create an original tall tale.

Glossary of Literary Terms

Alliteration: A repetition of initial, or beginning, sounds in two or more consecutive or neighboring words.

Analogy: A comparison based upon the resemblance in some particular ways between things that are otherwise unlike.

Anecdote: A short account of an interesting, amusing or biographical occurrence.

Anticlimax: An event that is less important than what occurred before it.

Archaic language: Language that was once common in a particular historic period but which is no longer commonly used.

Cause and effect: The relationship in which one condition brings about another condition as a direct result. The result, or consequence, is called the effect.

Character development: The ways in which the author shows how a character changes as the story proceeds.

Characterization: The method used by the author to give readers information about a character; a description or representation of a person's qualities or peculiarities.

Classify: To arrange according to a category or trait.

Climax: The moment when the action in a story reaches its greatest conflict.

Compare and contrast: To examine the likenesses and differences of two people, ideas or things. (*Contrast* always emphasizes differences. *Compare* may focus on likenesses alone or on likenesses and differences.)

Conflict: The main source of drama and tension in a literary work; the discord between persons or forces that brings about dramatic action.

Connotation: Something suggested or implied, not actually stated.

Description: An account that gives the reader a mental image or picture of something.

Dialect: A form of language used in a certain geographic region; it is distinguished from the standard form of the language by pronunciation, grammar and/or vocabulary.

Dialogue (dialog): The parts of a literary work that represent conversation.

Fact: A piece of information that can be proven or verified.

Figurative language: Description of one thing in terms usually used for something else. Simile and metaphor are examples of figurative language.

Flashback: The insertion of an earlier event into the normal chronological sequence of a narrative.

Foreshadowing: The use of clues to give readers a hint of events that will occur later on.

Historical fiction: Fiction represented in a setting true to the history of the time in which the story takes place.

Imagery: Language that appeals to the senses; the use of figures of speech or vivid descriptions to produce mental images.

Irony: The use of words to express the opposite of their literal meaning.

Legend: A story handed down from earlier times; its truth is popularly accepted but cannot be verified.

Limerick: A humorous five-lined poem with a specific form: aabba. Lines 1, 2 and 5 are longer than lines 3 and 4.

Metaphor: A figure of speech that compares two unlike things without the use of like or as.

Mood: The feeling that the author creates for the reader.

Motivation: The reasons for the behavior of a character.

Narrative: The type of writing that tells a story.

Narrator: The character who tells the story.

Opinion: A personal point of view or belief.

Parody: Writing that ridicules or imitates something more serious.

Personification: A figure of speech in which an inanimate object or an abstract idea is given human characteristics.

Play: A literary work that is written in dialogue form and that is usually performed before an audience.

Plot: The arrangement or sequence of events in a story.

Point of view: The perspective from which a story is told.

Protagonist: The main character.

Pun: A play on words that are similar in sound but different in meaning.

Realistic fiction: True-to-life fiction; the people, places and happenings are similar to those in real life.

Resolution: The part of the plot from the climax to the ending where the main dramatic conflict is worked out.

Satire: A literary work that pokes fun at individual or societal weaknesses.

Sequencing: The placement of story elements in the order of their occurrence.

Setting: The time and place in which the story occurs.

Simile: A figure of speech that uses *like* or *as* to compare two unlike things.

Stereotype: A character whose personality traits represent a group rather than an individual.

Suspense: Quality that causes readers to wonder what will happen next.

Symbolism: The use of a thing, character, object or idea to represent something else.

Synonyms: Words that are very similar in meaning.

Tall tale: An exaggerated story detailing unbelievable events.

Theme: The main idea of a literary work; the message the author wants to communicate, sometimes expressed as a generalization about life.

Tone: The quality or feeling conveyed by the work; the author's style or manner of expression.

ANSWERS

© 1995 Educational Impressions, Inc.

Pre-Reading Activity

1. venue	4. solicitor	7. defendant	10. contempt	13. verdict	16. convict
2. subpoena	5. litigant	8. testimony	11. evidence	14. acquittal	
3. jury	6. testify	9. cross-examine	12. prosecute	15. appeal	

Chapters One, Two, and Three: Vocabulary

1. D	4. J	7. L	10. E	13. H	16. F
2. G	5. P	8. A	11. O	14. C	17. K
3. N	6. R	9. Q	12. B	15. I	18. M

Chapter One: Comprehension and Discussion Questions (Answers may vary.)

1. The author used Scout Finch as first-person narrator. Scout tells the story in retrospect, beginning with events that occurred when she was six years old. In telling the story, Scout uses a great deal of realistic dialogue. This dialogue is in the present tense and gives readers the feeling that the story is unfolding before them. From the start, there is a sense of foreboding, for she begins by telling us that Jem was badly injured. We know that the events she is about to relate will lead to that injury!

2. The story takes place in the fictional town of Maycomb, Alabama. It begins in 1933. Although we are not actually told the year, there is a clue regarding President Franklin D. Roosevelt's 1933 inaugural address: "Maycomb County had recently been told that it had nothing to fear but fear itself."

3. It was the Depression. "There was no hurry, for there was nowhere to go, nothing to buy and no money to buy it with." Readers are told that tradition was very important in the South of that era. The short family history, so important in Southern tradition, was a source of shame to some members of the Finch family. Also, there have been several breaks with tradition: Atticus Finch had broken with tradition by leaving Finch's Landing. There is the sense that he might again break with tradition. Also breaking with tradition were the Radleys. A sense of mystery and foreboding was established with the description of the Radley home and the malevolent phantom! Readers are introduced to the prejudices that existed. "The sheriff hadn't the heart to put him [Boo] in jail alongside Negroes...." Another tradition of prejudice existed: the stereotyping of families. "But they were Haverfords, in Maycomb County a name synonymous with jackass."

4. The three role-played different characters from novels. When they got bored with that, Dill got the idea to try to get the recluse Boo Radley to come out of his house.

Chapter Two: Comprehension and Discussion Questions (Answers may vary.)

1. Satire is the use of wit, irony, or sarcasm to expose or ridicule a vice or folly. The author satirized education—specifically, the preoccupation with the processes of proper education. Miss Caroline was annoyed that Scout had learned to read and write before entering school. Also, she satirized a system that imposes values upon the students. As shown by her choice of story, the teacher did not relate to her students' culture.

2. Scout tried to explain to Miss Caroline why Walter couldn't accept her quarter. The Cunninghams were very proud. Although they couldn't pay for services with cash, they always paid back with goods. For example, Mr. Cunningham partially paid Atticus for his legal services with a load of stovewood.

3. Answers will vary, but she probably felt overwhelmed. She was trying her best to implement what she had been taught; however, she was in a new environment amongst people whose culture she did not understand.

Chapter Three: Comprehension and Discussion Questions (Answers may vary.)

1. Scout had a temper. She was quick to blame Walter for her problem in school and was ready to fight. Jem was more mature. He treated Walter kindly and with respect. Scout wasn't too tactful when she commented on Walter's eating habits. She said, "He's just a Cunningham." She was quick to label families.

2. In the first chapter, Scout said in regard to the events leading to Jem's injury, "I maintain that the Ewells started it all." In this chapter Little Chuck explained, "Ain't got no mother and their paw's right contentious."

3. Answers will vary.

4. Answers will vary, but the following should be included: She seemed intelligent. She taught Scout to write. She was well spoken, except when flustered. She was polite and treated others with respect and kindness. She was a strict disciplinarian and reprimanded Scout when Scout was rude to others. She seemed to be a big help to Atticus in raising the children. She had a great deal of affection for the children.

5. If Scout agreed that it was necessary to go to school, Atticus would continue to read with her every night.

Chapters Four, Five, and Six: Vocabulary

1. ramshakle	4. asinine	7. evasion	10. quibble	13. inquisitive
2. edification	5. pestilence	8. tacit	11. probate	14. auspicious
3. arbitrated	6. scuppernogs	9. parcel	12. contradicted	15. offended

Chapter Four: Comprehension and Discussion Questions (Answers may vary.)

1. Many will probably guess that Boo had been putting the gifts in the tree. Jem, too, probably suspected Boo. "He looked for a long time at the Radley Place. He seemed to be thinking again."

2. They were role-playing the Radleys. "It was a melancholy little drama, woven from bits and scraps of gossip and neighborhood legend." Jem probably knew that Atticus would object to their game. In Chapter One we learned that Atticus had told Jem to "mind his own business and let the Radleys mind theirs."

3. Scout had been anxious all along because she was afraid Boo would get them. She believed that Atticus knew what they had been doing. Also, she had heard laughing coming from the Radley house.

Chapter Five: Comprehension and Discussion Questions (Answers may vary.)

1. Jem and Dill had grown closer and were excluding Scout from many of their activities. A chameleon is a lizard capable of changing its color to blend with its environment. During the day Miss Maudie dressed in overalls and an old straw hat to work in her garden. In the evening she was transformed into a beautiful lady.

2. Miss Maudie said, "The things that happen to people we never really know. What happens behind closed doors, what secrets—" She wasn't referring to Atticus, but Scout felt it necessary to defend him. She said, "Atticus don't ever do anything to Jem and me in the house that he don't do in the yard."

3. Answers will vary.

4. Atticus caught the children in their attempt to get a note to Boo. Atticus warned them to stay away from the house unless invited. He also told them not to play their game nor make fun of anyone. He knew Jem would protest that they weren't making fun of Boo. Jem slipped and said, "We were just—" This gave it away that the game did, in fact, have to do with the Radleys.

Chapter Six: Comprehension and Discussion Questions (Answers may vary.)
1. Boo's brother Nathan apparently heard or saw them. According to Miss Maudie, he thought there was a "Negro in his collard patch" and shot in the air, frightening him away. Jem's pants got stuck on the fence and he had to leave them there.

2. This shows the willingness of the town to blame unexplained occurrences on Negroes.

3. Jem went although afraid because he didn't want to disappoint his father. He regretted what he had done.

Chapters Seven, Eight, and Nine: Vocabulary

1. deviation	5. behavior	9. incitement	13. promising	17. acquired
2. address	6. feature	10. pursue	14. indifferent	18. quiet
3. determine	7. commit	11. respectful	15. deceitful	19. flexible
4. payment	8. obtain	12. dissimilar	16. avoidable	20. understandable

Chapter Seven: Comprehension and Discussion Questions (Answers may vary.)
1. Jem's pants, which were all in a tangle and torn when he ran away, were now neatly folded and mended. It upset him because it meant someone had been expecting him and predicting his moves. Because they were sewn in a child-like manner, it was probably Boo who fixed and folded the pants. If so, it shows tenderness and caring on Boo's part toward the children.

2. The first two gifts were given in Chapter Four: 2 pieces of chewing gum and 2 polished pennies. In Chapter Seven, there were 5 more: a ball of gray twine, 2 dolls carved in soap, a package of gum, a medal, and a pocket watch.

3. Jem probably realized that Boo had been leaving the gifts. He was more mature than Scout and probably recognized the fact that Mr. Radley had taken away Boo's only means of communicating with them.

Chapter Eight: Comprehension and Discussion Questions (Answers may vary.)
1. Scout had never seen snow before.

2. He said "bad children" like Scout and Jem caused the seasons to change. He said it was written on the Rosetta Stone.

3. In 1799 a large black basalt tablet was found near Rosetta, Egypt. The tablet bore an inscription in Greek, Egyptian hieroglyphic, and Demotic (the native Egyptian of the time); it provided the key to the decipherment of hieroglyphics. The inscription itself was a decree passed by Egyptian priests and had nothing to do with children's behavior or the seasons.

4. In past chapters, we saw that Scout, although compassionate, basically repeated the superficial, stereotypical notions held by others in the town. She probably used the word because she heard others use it and didn't realize how hurtful it was.

5. They had created a caricature of Mr. Avery.

6. Boo Radley put the blanket around her. This reinforces the notion that he cared for the children and wanted to protect them.

7. She reacted with a sense of humor: "I'll have more room for my azaleas now!" She immediately made plans to build a new home that would suit her needs. Even with her problems, she was interested in others. She showed gratitude for those who had helped and she planned to bake a cake for Mr. Avery.

Chapter Nine: Comprehension and Discussion Questions (Answers may vary.)
1. Tom Robinson was a Negro accused of a crime. Atticus will be defending him. Many townspeople believed that Atticus shouldn't defend him.

2. Atticus knew that the children would hear "ugly talk" against him for defending Tom. He also knew that Scout had a temper and a willingness to fight when provoked.

3. Atticus knew that in the South of 1933, no jury would have taken the word of a black man against that of a white person. The prejudices were too deeply ingrained.

4. A *changeling* is a child secretly changed for another. Although brother and sister, Atticus and Alexandra were very different. Atticus didn't dwell on what Scout wore; Alexandra was "fanatical" on the subject of proper attire. Alexandra was concerned that Scout wasn't ladylike. Atticus was concerned with the way she treated others.

5. Francis, although the product of "proper upbringing," showed no compassion towards others. He spoke of Dill as a "runt" and called his uncle a "nigger-lover" because he was defending Tom Robinson. He blamed Scout for starting their fight. Scout didn't tell that he had provoked her because she wanted to spare Atticus's feelings.

6. "Scout's got to learn to keep her head and learn soon, with what's in store for her . . . ." "What bothers me is that she and Jem will have to absorb some ugly things soon." "It [the situation] couldn't be worse."

7. He was referring to prejudice.

Chapters Ten, Eleven, and Twelve: Vocabulary

1. feeble	3. tartly	5. rectitude	7. cantankerous	9. livid	11. tirade
2. inconspicuous	4. umbrage	6. interdict	8. propensity	10. compassion	12. melancholy

Chapter Ten: Comprehension and Discussion Questions (Answers may vary.)
1. His advice was to "shoot all the bluejays you want . . . but remember it's a sin to kill a mockingbird." As Miss Maudie explained, mockingbirds only make music for us; they do us no harm. The mockingbird symbolizes innocence.

2. Atticus was older than their friends' parents. He didn't partake in activities common to the other parents. For example, Jem was disappointed that Atticus wasn't going to play touch football with the other fathers. The children weren't very impressed by the things he was good at.

3. Atticus killed a mad dog with one shot. They learned that although Atticus never told them of his skill, he had a reputation for being an excellent shot.

4. Both admired Atticus's skill and courage. Scout was anxious to brag to everyone about it. Jem seemed to respect the fact that if Atticus had wanted to brag about this skill, he would have told them about it himself. Jem appreciated qualities such as modesty and compassion that made him a gentleman.

Chapter Eleven: Comprehension and Discussion Questions (Answers may vary.)

1. Mrs. Dubose denounced Atticus and the way he was bringing up his children. She said, "Your father's no better than the niggers and trash he works for!" Jem had gotten use to other children taunting them about Atticus's defense of Tom Robinson, but an adult doing it seemed to get to him. Most bothersome, however, seemed to be Mrs. Dubose's remarks about their mother.

2. A philippic is a verbal denunciation marked by abusive language. It is called such after the orations of Demosthenes against Philip of Macedonia in the fourth century B.C.

3. Scout had questioned Atticus's decision to defend Tom Robinson. Her feeling was that if most people thought he was wrong, maybe he was. Atticus tried to explain that he had to do what he thought was right. He had to let his conscience guide him or he wouldn't have been able to live with himself.

4. He would read to her after school for two hours a day for a period of a month.

5. He responded by taking it literally. He said that he was a "nigger-lover" because he tried to love everyone. He explained that although he thought the term was common and ugly, to him it was not an insult.

6. "Jem would gaze at Mrs. Dubose with a face devoid of resentment. Through the weeks he had cultivated an expression of polite and detached interest."

7. She had become addicted to morphine, which had been prescribed as a pain-killer by her doctors. She was determined to break the addiction before she died; she accomplished this goal.

8. Atticus said that courage was "when you know you're licked before you begin but you begin anyway and you see it through no matter what. You rarely win, but sometimes you do." Atticus was in a similar situation. He was defending Tom Robinson although he knew that he had little chance of winning.

Chapters Twelve, Thirteen, and Fourteen: Vocabulary

1. quarrel	4. abrupt	7. clothes	10. thinking	13. irritation
2. copies	5. persistence	8. hinder	11. right	
3. quarrelsome	6. awesome	9. unjust	12. doubt	

Chapter Twelve: Comprehension and Discussion Questions (Answers may vary.)

1. We learned that times were hard. "There were sit-down strikes in Birmingham; bread lines in the cities grew longer, people in the country grew poorer." Scout said that the events were remote from her world, but that wasn't really true. This boded poorly for Tom Robinson. When times are bad, people are more apt to blame other groups for their problems. They are more apt to use those groups as scapegoats.

2. "It was paid for from the first earnings of freed slaves." Calpurnia's son read the hymns line for line. After each line, the congregation sang out what Zeebo had read. This was called lining. Zeebo was the only one with a hymn-book, but even if they could have collected money for more books, most of the people in the congregation didn't know how to read.

3. Reverend Sykes wanted to collect $10.00 to help Tom Robinson's wife. The black community seemed to be close and willing to sacrifice to help one another.

4. She didn't want others to think she was acting superior to them. She believed it would annoy them. This was similar to Miss Maudie's statement in Chapter Ten regarding the fact that Atticus didn't brag about his shooting ability: "People in their right minds never take pride in their talents."

Chapter Thirteen: Comprehension and Discussion Questions (Answers may vary.)

1. Atticus said, "I can't stay here all day with you, and the summer's going to be a hot one." Although Scout didn't understand his meaning, readers got the feeling that he wasn't referring to the weather!

2. This was so unlike their father that they almost felt as if they had lost him. He was mouthing the words of Alexandra.

3. "It's not time to worry" gave us the feeling that eventually it will be that time!

Chapter Fourteen: Comprehension and Discussion Questions (Answers may vary.)

1. Alexandra was referring to Calpurnia. She wanted him to get rid of her; she thought they didn't need her. Alexandra probably objected to Calpurnia's influence over the children. Atticus reacted by saying that Calpurnia was like a member of the family, that she had been a positive influence on the children, and that the children loved her.

2. He told Atticus that Dill was hiding under the bed.

3. Dill was filthy. Atticus wanted him to get cleaned up.

4. Dill felt that his parents weren't interested in him. He believed that they gave him things in order to get him out of their way. Scout couldn't understand this because she believed that Atticus and Calpurnia—and even Jem—depended greatly on her.

5. Answers will vary, but Dill had an unstable, unhappy family life. In this chapter, he literally ran away. His tall tales were probably another means of escape from reality.

Chapters Fifteen, Sixteen, and Seventeen

1. E	4. F	7. C	10. E	13. D	16. A	19. A
2. F	5. A	8. H	11. A	14. G	17. E	20. A
3. A	6. C	9. B	12. C	15. F	18. A	21. E

Chapter Fifteen: Comprehension and Discussion Questions (Answers may vary.)

1. He probably realized that sentiments would be the same wherever they took it in the state.

2. "It's that Old Sarum bunch I'm worried about...." set us up for the appearance of the mob.

3. Jem had sensed that something was wrong when the men were outside the Finch home. He noticed that Atticus had taken the car although he almost always walked. Jem was afraid that someone would hurt Atticus.

4. Both groups objected to Atticus's defense of Tom Robinson. The first group of men remained calm and friendly. Although they didn't want Atticus to defend Tom, they also seemed to want to avoid trouble rather than cause it. They came to warn Atticus rather than to threaten him. The second crowd of men behaved more like a mob. They tried to hide from view so that they wouldn't be recognized. They obviously came to get Tom Robinson. They treated Jem roughly and spoke to Atticus in a threatening manner.

5. Scout recognized a member of the mob and innocently began a conversation about his son, who was in Scout's class. She went on to discuss other matters she thought would interest him. We were told earlier that the members of the mob were trying to hide. When individuals are part of a mob, they lose some of their sense of personal responsibility. Scout broke the ''mob mentality'' by addressing Mr. Cunningham as an individual—not as a member of the mob. Once Mr. Cunningham became an individual, he was ashamed of his behavior. He then helped break up the rest of the mob.

6. Atticus was proud of Jem. He knew that Jem was trying to protect him and that he was standing by his convictions.

Chapter Sixteen: Comprehension and Discussion Questions (Answers may vary.)
1. Jem knew that Scout was upset, so he took her into his room to sleep. He tried to reassure her that it would all be over soon. He didn't tease her about crying.

2. William Jennings Bryan (1860-1925), a lawyer and political leader, was considered by many to be the finest American orator ever.

3. The ancient Romans used to find it entertaining to watch the gladiators fight to their death. She felt that it was morbid to make a gala occasion out of a trial which would most likely end in a man's death.

4. Sarcasm is a mocking or ironic statement. Miss Maudie said, ''Better be careful he doesn't hand you a subpoena.'' She was mocking the fact that Miss Stephanie acted like she knew so much about the case (all of her information based on rumors). If she truly knew first hand all that she repeated, she could have been called as a witness!

5. She learned that the court had appointed Atticus to defend Tom Robinson. If she had known that, she would have used that fact in Atticus's defense. Scout didn't understand why the people were so upset with him as he didn't really have a choice.

6. They sat with Reverend Sykes in the ''colored balcony.''

Chapter Seventeen: Comprehension and Discussion Questions (Answers may vary.)
1. Answers will vary, but most will probably say that there was no medical proof that the crime was actually committed. Also, it seemed as if they weren't really concerned about her condition.

2. Answers will vary, but some will probably guess that a left-handed person had beaten Mayella and that Tom Robinson was right-handed.

3. They lived on public assistance, even in good economic times. The children were dirty and did not attend school. Their home surroundings were also filthy. They lived behind a garbage dump. Every day they picked through the garbage to see what they could use. Trash was strewn around their home. Mr. Ewell was crude and unrefined, as shown by his testimony. (In an earlier chapter, we saw that his son Burris was also rude.)

4. Atticus wanted to show that Mr. Ewell was left-handed.

5. She was afraid that he was asking a question of the witness without knowing in advance what to expect. She remembered the tenet Atticus had drummed into her head: ''Never...on cross-examination ask a witness a question you don't already know the answer to.''

Chapter Eighteen: Comprehension and Discussion Questions (Answers may vary.)
1. ''Mayella looked as if she tried to keep clean.'' She was probably responsible for the geraniums in their yard.

2. She wasn't used to being referred to as Miss Mayella and ma'am. She mistook Atticus's courtesy for mocking.

3. Tom Robinson's left arm had been totally disabled as the result of a childhood accident.

4. He believed that Bob Ewell had beaten her. The following questions asked by Atticus pointed in that direction: ''Except when he's drinking?'' (In response to ''He does tollable, 'cept when—'') ''Has he [your father] ever beaten you?'' ''Or didn't you scream until you saw your father...?'' ''Who beat you up? Tom Robinson or your father?'' ''Didn't Bob Ewell beat you up?''

5. Answers will vary, but Mayella's failure to answer the questions about whether it was really her father who beat her up suggested that she was lying.

Chapter Nineteen: Comprehension and Discussion Questions (Answers may vary.)
1. He was kind and compassionate. He did chores for Mayella because he knew she didn't get any help at home. He didn't accept money for the work because he knew she couldn't afford it.

2. Mayella seemed not to belong anywhere. She didn't even know the meaning of the word ''friends.'' When Atticus was polite to her, she thought he was making fun of her. Tom Robinson had probably been the only person to be nice to her.

3. Mayella's Testimony: She asked Tom to come inside to chop a chiffarobe. She had never asked him to come inside before then. She *might* have asked him to do jobs. Tom got behind her, and when she turned around, he choked her. She fought. He hit her over and over and ''took advantage'' of her. Her father came in and asked who did it. She fainted; when she came to, the sheriff was there.
Tom's Testimony: She had asked him to come inside to do chores several times. He never went inside without being asked. On November 21, she asked him to come inside to fix a door. She had sent the children to town. She grabbed him and jumped on him, hugging him. She kissed his face. He tried to run, but didn't want to push her. He ran away when Mr. Ewell came.

4. Link Deas, Tom's employer, spoke without the court's permission in Tom's behalf.

5. Tom said that he felt sorry for her. The prejudiced white community resented a black man feeling sorry for any white woman, no matter what her circumstances were.

6. He started to cry because of the way Mr. Gilmer spoke to Tom. It upset him that he called him ''boy.'' When Scout said, ''He's just a Negro,'' Dill said that it didn't matter—that no one had a right to speak to him that way.

Chapter Twenty: Comprehension and Discussion Questions (Answers may vary.)

1. He had the reputation of being a drunk. In reality, his sack contained Coca-Cola. He said people would never be able to understand that he just preferred to live with the Negroes.

2. He overheard Dill's disgust at the way Tom had been treated. He was touched that Dill could still cry about the mistreatment of one human being by another. He was pessimistic in that he believed that in a few years Dill would become hardened and would no longer be moved to tears.

3. Answers will vary.

4. Her society was a highly segregated one. She broke that society's code of separatism by kissing a Negro.

5. The evil assumption was that all Negroes are immoral. Atticus pointed out that there are some bad in every race.

6. "Distaff" refers to the female line of a family. Because the year was 1935, we know that he was referring to First Lady Eleanor Roosevelt.

7. Although people are unequal in many ways, they are supposed to be equal in the eyes of the law. Atticus realized, however, that a court is only as good as the individuals on the jury.

8. Answers will vary, but some might guess that they noticed that the children were missing.

Chapter Twenty-One: Comprehension and Discussion Questions (Answers may vary.)

1. Jem believed Atticus had proved beyond doubt that Tom Robinson was innocent. He was naive enough to believe the jurors would make the right decision. When Atticus said it would be over soon, Jem assumed the jury would quickly acquit Tom.

2. Everything in the courtroom was still. No one was talking. It reminded her of the incident with the mad dog when "the trees were still, the mockingbirds were silent, the carpenters...had vanished." In the earlier incident Mr. Tate had broken the silence by saying, "Take him, Mr. Finch." Now he broke the silence by saying, "This court will come to order."

3. "A jury never looks at a defendant it has convicted, and when this jury came in, not one of them looked at Tom Robinson."

4. Those in the Colored Balcony stood in respect as Atticus passed. He wanted her to do the same.

Chapter Twenty-Two: Comprehension and Discussion Questions (Answers may vary.)

1. In Chapter 20, Dolphus told them his secret because Dill could still cry over such inhumanity. "Let him get a little older and he won't get sick and cry. Maybe things'll strike him as ...not quite right...but he won't cry." In this chapter Atticus made a similar pessimistic observation. "They've done it before and they did it tonight and they'll do it again and when they do it—seems that only children weep."

2. He planned to appeal.

3. She invited the three children to her home for cake. She put out only two small cakes and cut Jem a slice from the big cake, setting him apart from the other two.

4. The black community stood beside him. Mr. Tate treated him fairly and told only the truth as he knew it. Judge Taylor helped by appointing Atticus rather than Maxwell Green to defend Tom.

5. She believed it was a good sign that the jury took so long to arrive at a verdict. "Atticus Finch [is] only man in these parts who can keep the jury out so long in a case like that....We're making a step."

6. She told them that Bob Ewell had spit at Atticus and had threatened to get revenge.

Chapter Twenty-Three: Comprehension and Discussion Questions (Answers may vary.)

1. In Chapter 3, Atticus had given Scout advice on how to get along with her teacher. "You never really understand a person until you consider things from his point of view...until you climb into his skin and walk around in it." In this chapter he asked Jem to stand in Bob Ewell's shoes. He explained that he had destroyed Bob Ewell's credibility and that Bob Ewell had to have some sort of comeback. Atticus was glad he took it out on him and not on his children.

2. "He did have deep misgivings when...the jury gave a death penalty on purely circumstantial evidence."

3. It dawned on Jem that most juries came from the back woods rather than from town. "For some reason he [Atticus] looked pleased with Jem. 'I was wondering when that'd occur to you,' " he said.

4. He told him that one of the Cunninghams tried to hold out for an acquittal.

5. She called Walter trash and she said Scout was a problem to her father.

Chapters Twenty-Four, Twenty-Five, Twenty-Six, and Twenty-Seven: Vocabulary

Part I			Part II		
1. c	4. a	7. b	1. Dif./a	4. Dif./b	7. Same
2. b	5. b	8. c	2. Same	5. Dif./a	8. Dif./a
3. a	6. c	9. b	3. Dif./b	6. Dif./b	9. Same

Chapter Twenty-Four: Comprehension and Discussion Questions (Answers may vary.)

1. The ladies showed concern and compassion for the distant tribe but not for people in their own town.

2. Mrs. Robinson didn't need forgiving. If anyone needed forgiving, it was Mayella for what she had done to Tom.

3. Mrs. Merriweather had been talking—without mentioning his name—about Atticus. "Some of 'em in this town thought they were doing the right thing...but all they did was stir 'em up." In response, Miss Maudie said to her, "His [Atticus's] food doesn't stick going down, does it?"

4. Miss Stephanie had asked her if she wanted to become a lawyer and then added sarcastically, "...I thought you wanted to be a lawyer, you've already commenced going to court."

5. He wanted Calpurnia to go with him to tell Mrs. Robinson that her husband had been killed trying to escape.

6. Answers will vary.

7. In past chapters Aunt Alexandra seemed primarily interested in "family background." Now she stood up for Atticus and showed concern for his welfare. She believed the town had been using him to do their dirty work and risking his health.

8. Scout showed new admiration for her aunt. She appreciated her aunt's deep feelings for Atticus. When Aunt Alexandra composed herself and resumed her activities as hostess, Scout did the same.

Chapter Twenty-Five: Comprehension and Discussion Questions (Answers may vary.)

1. Jem didn't want Scout to kill the insect because it didn't do anyone any harm. A principal theme of the book is the senseless, cruel behavior we often show to one another and the need for compassion.

2. Mr. Underwood "likened Tom's death to the senseless slaughter of songbirds by hunters and children."

3. The courts are supposed to treat each person equally, but as Atticus said in his closing remarks (Chapter 20), "a court is no better than each man of you sitting before me on this jury." Atticus had no chance to get an acquittal. It was the word of a black man against that of a white woman, and in the South of that time, the black man didn't stand a chance.

4. We learned that Mr. Ewell made a threatening remark: "It [Tom's death] made it one down and two more to go."

Chapter Twenty-Six: Comprehension and Discussion Questions (Answers may vary.)

1. She remembered the stunts she, Jem, and Dill had pulled trying to get a peek at Boo. She realized that it was cruel.

2. Although she expounded on the ills of persecuting one group of people, she encouraged prejudice against another. In reference to the guilty verdict, she had said, "It's time somebody taught 'em a lesson...."

3. It was too painful for Jem to think about it. Jem knew that Atticus had proved Tom's innocence, and he still couldn't accept the outcome. When enough time passes, he will probably be able to face what had happened.

Chapter Twenty-Seven: Comprehension and Discussion Questions (Answers May Vary)

1. He was fired by the WPA from a job; he was unsuccessful in his attempt to burglarize Judge Taylor's home; and Link Deas stopped him from harassing Helen Robinson.

2. He was referring to the Supreme Court.

3. We were told that Scout's costume would be uncomfortable and difficult to get out of, that Aunt Alexandra had a "pinprick of apprehension," and that the "longest journey" of the children's lives was about to begin.

Chapters Twenty-Eight, Twenty-Nine, Thirty, and Thirty-One: Vocabulary

1. irascible	4. garish	7. disengage	10. connive	13. squander	16. rale
2. pinion	5. untrammeled	8. persevere	11. instinctive	14. hock	
3. smocking	6. blandly	9. teeming	12. lectern	15. rout	

It is a sin to kill a mockingbird.

Chapter Twenty-Eight: Comprehension and Discussion Questions (Answers may vary.)

1. It was Halloween, a spooky time. There was talk of "haints." It was pitch black. "The street light...cast sharp shadows on the Radley house." Jem heard noises he couldn't identify. Scout couldn't change into her dress. Jem told her to be quiet, a sign that he was afraid. Scout thought it might be the wind rustling the trees, but realized there was no wind and only one tree. The noises didn't stop when the children stopped.

2. Scout thought it was because she was distracted. More likely, it was because Aunt Alexandra realized that Scout had been through a traumatic experience and wanted to make her feel more comfortable.

3. Answers will vary, but many will probably guess that it was Boo. They will probably remember that Boo had put a blanket on Scout to keep her warm during the fire at Miss Maudie's and that he had fixed Jem's pants.

4. "He's got a bump on the head...and a broken arm." He was unconscious for a while. When he started to come to, Dr. Reynolds gave him something to put him out again.

5. He revealed that Bob Ewell was dead at the scene. He had been killed with a kitchen knife.

Chapter Twenty-Nine: Comprehension and Discussion Questions (Answers may vary.)

1. In spite of the fact that she had had a bad feeling about that night, Aunt Alexandra had declined to accompany the children.

2. Scout explained that she knew she was under a tree because Jem had taught her that the ground was cooler under a tree. Mr. Tate was impressed by Jem's power of observation.

3. Boo Radley had brought him into the house.

Chapter Thirty: Comprehension and Discussion Questions (Answers may vary.)

1. She called him by his real name; guided him through the house; and offered him a chair on the porch, where he'd be at ease.

2. Atticus thought Jem had killed Bob Ewell in self-defense.

3. Boo Radley had killed him. This was evidenced by the fact that there were two knives.

4. The kitchen knife, used to kill Bob Ewell, was Boo's. The switchblade was Bob Ewell's. Mr. Tate wanted to protect Boo. He knew that Boo had only wanted to save the children and that it would be harmful to put him through a trial.

5. In Chapter 9 Atticus had told the children that they shouldn't use their air-rifles to shoot mockingbirds because mockingbirds make music for us to enjoy and do nothing to harm us. Scout analogized and compared putting Boo through the hardships of a trial to the killing of a mockingbird. Like the mockingbird, Boo represented innocence. He had shown kindness to the children on several instances and had done nothing to harm anyone.

Chapter Thirty-One: Comprehension and Discussion Questions (Answers May Vary)

1. She again called him by his given name. Rather than lead him to his house like a child, she put her hand into the crook of his arm so that he would appear to be escorting her if anyone—such as Miss Stephanie Crawford—was watching.

2. The Gray Ghost symbolized Boo. "An' they chased him 'n never could catch him...an' Atticus, when they finally saw him, why he hadn't done any of those things...Atticus, he was real nice...."

3. She stood on the Radley porch and viewed the surroundings from Boo's point of view.

Spotlight Literary Skill: Theme

THE NEED FOR HUMAN COMPASSION: The lack of and need for human compassion was shown primarily, but not exclusively, in regards to racism. Mr. Underwood editorialized about the shooting of Tom, a helpless, innocent creature who was destroyed because of prejudice and racism. He compared his killing to the senseless killing of songbirds. Scout noted: "in the secret courts of men's hearts Atticus had no case." The lack of human compassion caused Tom's death.

The author satirized the lack of and need for compassion in her description of Mrs. Merriweather's concern for the Mrunas and Mrs. Gates's concern for the treatment of the Jews by Hitler. Neither showed compassion for the blacks in their own country. Dolphus Raymond commented on the lack of compassion too: "Cry about the hell white people give colored folks, without even stopping to think that they're people too."

The lack of and need for human compassion was revealed in the plot revolving around Boo Radley. Boo was also a gentle, innocent creature. People were cruel to him in the stories they spread. The children, too, were cruel and insensitive. As time went on, however, they came to see the insensitivity of their behavior and began to treat him with compassion.

THE IMPORTANCE OF INDIVIDUAL CONSCIENCE: Atticus was a wonderful role model for his children. Scout asked Atticus why he was defending Tom Robinson if people thought he shouldn't. He responded, "The main one [reason] is, if I didn't I couldn't hold up my head in town, I couldn't represent this county...I couldn't even tell you or Jem not to do something again." He later said, "This case...is something that goes to the essence of a man's conscience...I couldn't go to church and worship God if I didn't try to help that man." When Scout noted that he must be wrong because most folks thought he was wrong, he responded, "Before I can live with other folks I've got to live with myself. The one thing that doesn't abide by majority rule is a person's conscience." When Atticus believed that Jem had killed Bob Ewell, he insisted that Jem be brought before the court. "If this thing's hushed up it'll be a simple denial to Jem of the way I've tried to raise him."

Spotlight Literary Skill: Symbolism

The mockingbird symbolizes harmless, gentle people such as Tom and Boo, who are often destroyed by the insensitive, cruel behavior of others.

1. In Chapter 10 Atticus advised, "Shoot all the bluejays you want...but remember it's a sin to kill a mockingbird." Miss Maudie concurred: "Mockingbirds don't do one thing but make music for us to enjoy."

2. In that same chapter it was noted that there were no mockingbirds singing as the mad dog neared.

3. In Chapter 25 Mr. Underwood wrote an editorial in which "he likened Tom's death to the senseless slaughter of songbirds by hunters and children."

4. In Chapter 28 the mockingbird was used to symbolize Boo Radley. As Scout and Jem passed the Radley home on the way to the pageant, they heard a mockingbird.

5. In Chapter 30 Mr. Tate noted that it would be a sin to make Boo, with all his shy ways, to go through the ordeal of a trial. Scout pointed out that "it'd be sort of like shootin' a mockingbird."

Character Quest

1. Miss Caroline said it to Scout because Atticus had taught Scout to read. She wanted her to learn by the proper method.

2. Calpurnia said it to Scout because Scout had commented adversely on Walter's eating habits while a guest in their home.

3. Atticus said it to Scout. Scout was upset with the way Miss Caroline had treated her. Atticus told her she'd get along better with people if she learned to look at things from their point of view.

4. Mr. Avery said it to Jem and Scout. He blamed them for the unusual snowfall.

5. Atticus said it to Jem and Scout when he gave them their air-rifles. He didn't want them to harm gentle, innocent creatures.

6. Atticus said it to Jem about Mrs. Dubose. She was a morphine addict and was determined to break herself of the habit before she died. She accomplished this seemingly hopeless feat.

7. Tom Robinson said it to Mr. Gilmer when questioned about why he had helped Mayella without getting paid.

8. Dolphus Raymond said it to Scout, Jem, and Dill. He was referring to Dill's feeling sick about Tom's treatment.

9. Heck Tate said it to Atticus. He was explaining why he would report that Bob Ewell had fallen on his own knife rather than report the fact that Arthur Radley had killed him.

Crossword Puzzle

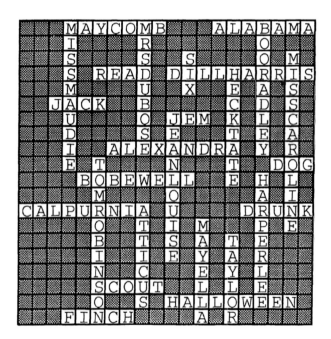